# Social Work Day

## International Congress of Qualitative Inquiry

## Official Program

Illini Union
University of Illinois
Urbana, Illinois, USA
Thursday, 17 May 2018

Social Work Day is the great qualitative social work get-together. Held each May at the International Congress of Qualitative Inquiry (ICQI) in Urbana, IL, USA, Social Work Day attracts researchers from throughout the world. This is the premier international qualitative social work conference where scholars present cutting edge research using both traditional and innovative qualitative research methods.

Norman Denzin is the director of ICQI, Dr. Denzin is emeritus Distinguished Professor of Communications, College of Communications Scholar, and Research Professor of Communications, Sociology, and Humanities, University of Illinois, Urbana-Champaign, USA.

Jane Gilgun is the organizer of Social Work Day. Dr. Gilgun is professor, School of Social Work, University of Minnesota, Twin Cities, USA.

The papers are organized into panels based primarily on methods and methodologies.

Please note that Room 210 is on the ballroom side of the Union and getting there requires using the staircase or elevator on the far side of the Union.

Cover Photo: Valley in County Donegal, Ireland, by Jane Gilgun

ISBN-13: 978-1987615357
ISBN-10: 1987615352

# Social Work Day
### Thursday, 17 May 2018

## Theme: Qualitative Inquiry in Troubled Times
*Jane F. Gilgun, University of Minnesota, Twin Cities, Organizer*

**8:00-8:30**                                                                 **Illini Room A**
### Welcome & Introductions

**8:30-9:20**
### 1256371 Opening Plenary: Social Work and the Common Good

*Jane F. Gilgun, PhD, University of Minnesota, Chair*

Social work has a common vision while welcoming multiple perspectives. In this roundtable plenary session, three social work researchers with three social locations will share their visions for their research. They will address issues such as what social locations do I occupy? Why is my research important? What impact do I want my research to have? What do I do to ensure that my research has impact? After their presentation, participants will share their own visions for their research.

Anindita Bhattacharya, Columbia University
Christine Mayor, Wilfrid Laurier University
Austin Oswald, City University of New York
Burcu Ozturk, University of Alabama

**9:30-10:50**
### Concurrent Sessions

### 1383164 Round Robin on Topics in Social Work Research
*Cesar Cisneros-Puebla, Autonomous Metropolitan University, Chair*
Union 210

This session will be a round robin, meaning we will set up four stations for four different topics. Persons knowledgeable about the topics will be at each station. Participants at the session will visit each station for 15 minutes and engage in dialogue with the knowledgeable person(s) and each other. After 15 minutes, participants will move to the next station. Topics include content analysis, writing for publication, being white while doing reseach with African Americans, and a narrative autobiographical approach to data analysis

o   Jim Drisko, Smith College, Content Analysis
o   Sondra Fogel, University of South Florida, Writing for Publication
o   Thomas Kenemore, Loyola University Chicago, Being White While Doing Reseach with African Americans
o   Cesar Cisneros-Puebla, Autonomous Metropolitan University, & Vanessa Jara-Labarth, University of Tarapac, A Narrative Autobiographical Approach to Data Analysis

**Workshop: Facilitators and Barriers to Using Participatory
Action Research Among Early Career Social Work Scholars**
*Darren Cosgrove & Catherine S. Kramer; dcosgrove@albany.edu; ckramer@albany.edu*
Union 314 A

Participatory action research and community-based participatory research offer opportunities for social work scholars to conduct research that addresses complex social issues. However, these methodologies often require researchers to navigate unique challenges and tensions, especially for scholars working within institutional settings that privilege traditional forms of research. This workshop is intended for social work doctoral students and early career faculty (< 5 years of experience) who are committed to practicing these methodologies or have wished to practice them and did not (for any reason). Session attendees will participate in a study intended to identify and document the facilitators and barriers that new and emerging social work scholars encounter when practicing PAR and CBPR. The findings from this research will be published to benefit the broader social work community. Participants will engage in group-based activities and discussions designed to identify common challenges and opportunities. Through sharing and reflecting, participants will make insights and identify pathways.

**Grounded Theory and Policy-Focused Research**
*Verena Schmidt, University of Louisville, Chair*
Union 314 B

1371067 **Applied Educational Neuroscience Practices in Classrooms: A Grounded Theory Study** *Sheila Dennis, Indiana University & Susan Lynn Glassburn Larimer, Indiana University; dennis2@iupui.edu; slarimer@iupui.edu*

Educational neuroscience is an emerging discipline seeking to meld psychology, education, and the neurosciences. This grounded theory study explored the process of operationalizing educational neuroscience principles in the classroom in order to better inform interactions between teachers, school social workers, administrators, and students. The research questions were: (1) How do teachers, school administrators, and students describe educational neuroscience? (2) What practices do teachers use in the classroom to apply educational neuroscience principles? (3) How do students respond to their practices? (4) What classroom interactions are associated with these practices? The results of this translational study will inform educational and school social work practice regarding co-regulation, attachment, and intersubjective meaning-making in the classroom context. Findings also contribute questions for further discourse surrounding the transdisciplinary vision of bridging objective science and the heuristic ways of knowing inherent in direct educational and school social work practices.

1370107 **Relational Qualitative Methods in Community-Engaged Health Research with Refugees** *Jessica Euna Lee, Indiana University; jel6@iu.edu*

This paper discusses ethical and methodological considerations for community-engaged research with refugee communities. This presentation explains the interviewing and participant recruitment processes of a study examining health care utilization among Bhutanese refugees in one U.S. city during the postresettlement period. Findings from this study suggest that language, culture, social networks, health systems, and prior experiences with health care interact with each other and inform Bhutanese refugees' health care utilization processes. These findings are relevant to interventions and policies for refugees worldwide. Using grounded theory methods, data were gathered through interviews with Bhutanese refugee adults. This study exercised relational constructivist approaches by formulating the study's research questions, instrument, and recruitment strategy in consultation with refugee community members. A relational constructivist stance enables collaboration between researchers and participants, which promotes participatory approaches in cross-cultural research. This study carries implications for providers and researchers working with refugees.

1368507 **Forensic Interviewer Response to Non-/Partial Disclosure in Sexually Abused Children** *Emily A. Lux, University of Illinois at Urbana-Champaign; ealux@illinois.edu*

Children who have experienced trauma, have contact with child protective services, and who have experienced sexual abuse are shown to be at higher risks for developmental delays and disturbances in memory and cognition. These impediments could potentially impair a child's ability to articulate clear details about any sexual abuse they endured. Forensic interviewers who collect information from these children are in unique situations in balancing the need to elicit accurate and sufficient testimony to protect sexually abused children while not suggestively coercing a statement from the child. This qualitative study uses grounded theory to explore how forensic interviewers use interviewing protocols and multidisciplinary teams when interviewing non-/partial disclosure in children who are suspected of experiencing sexual abuse, as well as how the forensic interviewer defends these practices as an expert witness in court-related scenarios. Overarching themes from 20-30 face-to-face interviews with forensic interviewers will be presented based on preliminary findings.

1368372 **Incarceration Experiences of Older African American Adults Living with HIV** *Verena Schmidt, University of Louisville; v0schm01@louisville.edu*

Two epidemics disproportionally impact older (aged 50+ years) African Americans compared to the general U.S. population: Incarceration and HIV/AIDS. The purpose of this constructivist grounded theory study was to understand the incarceration experiences of older African Americans living with HIV (AAPLWHA). This study had three main questions: 1) What are the incarceration experiences of older AAPLWHA? 2) How do older AAPLWHA draw meaning from their incarceration experiences? 3) How do incarceration experiences and understandings of their meaning relate to engagement in care? Twenty two older AAPLWHA with incarceration histories participated in qualitative interviews, and seven participants were selected for in-depth qualitative follow up interviews. Constructivist Grounded Theory techniques were used to analyze the qualitative data. Through the exploration of participants' incarceration experiences, four themes emerged: 1) HIV care and treatment; 2) "special rules" for HIV positive inmates; 3) multi-layered, intersectional stigma within the correctional environment and 4) linkage of HIV care post-release.

## Theorizing Unexplored Experiences Through Reflexivity
*Austin Oswald, City University of New York, Chair*
Union 404

### 1373979 A Reflexive Exploration in Qualitative Team Research
*Samantha Clarke, Wilfrid Laurier University; sam.clarke@rogers.com*

Examining power is intrinsic to social work and seems inescapable in academia, and so I seek to deconstruct shifting and contentious issues of power and the epistemological invisibility that I encountered in a qualitative group research project Qualitative research offers ways to minimize power differentials through an interrogation of invisible and unexplored assumptions. It may also further embed that which it seeks to uncover if researchers are not purposeful in its use. Unable to untangle the knot of critical insights produced by the usual reflexive process, I use poetry as a reflexive healing device to explore my learning throughout this research project.

### 1383185 From the Inside Out: Reflexivity in a Graduate Capstone Course
*Cray Mulder, Grand Valley State University; muldecra@gvsu.edu*

As MSW social work students frequently prioritize the development of micro practice skills and clinical roles post-graduation, they may wrestle with how to best incorporate research findings and methods into practice. This paper proposes a reflexive approach to an MSW capstone course, whereby the instructor presented reflexivity to students at the beginning of the semester as the framework for the course. Throughout this final MSW course students examined themselves as social workers, different facets of their professional identity, and how the literature about reflexivity applied to their professional conceptualizations at the end of a graduate program. Moreover, students applied a reflexive approach to case presentations and analyses, ethical dilemmas and their understandings of social justice. In addition to heightened self-awareness and preparation for professional practice, this approach integrated constructs of qualitative inquiry as the foundation for a non-research methods course further linking research and practice.

1370423 **Writing Survivor Stories: Using Qualitative Inquiry to Understand the Long-Term Impact of Sexual Violence** *Andrea Nikischer, SUNY Buffalo State; nikiscab@buffalostate.edu*

Recent revelations of wide-spread sexual harassment, misconduct and assault from men in power in the media and U.S. government have grabbed headlines and ended careers. While much attention has been given to the perpetrators of this sexual violence, there has been little discussion of the potential long-term impact of such violence on the lives of survivors. This presentation will describe a qualitative interview method, Ethnographic Longitudinal Reflection (ELR), created specifically to unravel the complex series of challenges and choices survivors face post-sexual assault and to further understand the ways that sexual assault can impact education and career goalsetting and achievement. ELR privileges the voices of survivors, empowering them to write their own stories about the long-term impact of sexual violence. Detailed information about the ELR method will be shared and findings from an ELR research study with eight survivors of sexual assault will be discussed.

1357364 **Complex Intimacy: Theorizing Older Gay Men's Social Lives** *Austin Oswald, City University of New York; aoswald@gradcenter.cuny.edu*

This qualitative study provides an in-depth exploration into the social lives of older gay men. In-depth interviews were conducted with 10 gay men over the age of 65 to elicit details about their relationships with other people. Findings paint a complex picture of older gay social life that is compounded by significant events affecting the personal and collective gay man. Three overarching themes emerged that capture the social lives of the participants: i) Coming of age as a gay man in the 20th century; ii) Dealing with the aging body; and iii) Enduring loss and the consequent impact on social life. The participants reported that being in a gay environment and closing the gay generational divide helped them adjust to their changing social lives in later life. This study adds to an ongoing discussion about the experiences of older gay men and makes suggestions for future research and practice.


**11:00-12:20**

**Concurrent Sessions**

**Axes of Identity and Reflexivity in Research and Practice**
*David Camacho, Columbia University, Chair*
Union 210

1383693 **Unpacking Privilege and Resistance: Building Competence to Serve Marginalized Populations through Narrative Inquiry** *Tracie Rogers, University of the Southern Caribbean; tracie.rogers@gmail.com*

This paper discusses the engagement of undergraduate social work students in transformative social justice education through the use of arts-based research practice. The HIV epidemic, oppression of sexual minority groups and upsurge in gender-based violence are striking features of our lived experience in the Caribbean. As a result, the ability to competently work with marginalized groups is a requirement for all social workers. Using transcript data from four interviewees belonging to marginalized populations, students engaged in qualitative analysis and intensive reflective dialogue. Based on these interactions with the data, students also created fictional narratives aimed at accessing and presenting multiple viewpoints of marginalized identities. The researcher will present findings of how engaging with story and story-making builds core components of professional self-awareness necessary for competent social work practice. The presentation hones in research methodology as well as how students grapple with their personal identities and meaning-making around marginalization.

**1371339 Growing up in Impoverished Households: Low-Income Single Mothers' Narratives** *Tumani Malinga, University of Illinois at Urbana-Champaign; malinga2@illinois.edu*

Although Botswana women are vulnerable, there is little research on their lived experiences. In this paper, the author focuses on women's narratives about their upbringing in rural Botswana. Utilizing a narrative research approach, face-to-face interviews were conducted with fifteen low-income single Botswana mothers. Thematic analysis was undertaken of women's narratives to understand the household environment they grew up in and how it influenced their lives. Growing up in impoverished households was common for the participants. They narrated that growing up in resource deprived households exposed them to more hardships and accumulation of subsequent life disadvantages later in life, impacting on their life quality and trajectories. Children growing up in at risk families need to be provided with necessary support to ensure that they benefit from educational opportunities. Also, enhancing early family relationships that can buffer childhood adversities is an important intervention to help women onto healthier trajectories.

**1371311 Embodied Tableaux: Drama-Based Arts-Based Resarch Methodology in Social Work Research** *Christine Mayor, Wilfrid Laurier University; mayo6830@mylaurier.ca*

This presentation will focus on the use of drama and embodiment techniques in arts-based methodology (ABR) for social work research. Specifically, this presentation will focus on the adaptation of drama therapy tableaux exercises and Augusto Boal's (1992) Image Theatre for data generation and data analysis when working with focus groups. Blending techniques from the presenter's career as a drama therapist with her current research and studies in social work, this presentation will provide attendees with concrete steps for utilizing drama techniques in their own research. In order to highlight how this method might be implemented, the presentation will include samples from the data generation (i.e. pictures of focus group tableaux) and analysis from a recent study conducted on the roles and tools needed when working clinically in the school system.

1384104 **Exploring Sexual Minority Men's Experiences of Depression: A Comprehensive Meta-Synthesis** *David Camacho, Columbia University, Ellen Lukens, Columbia University School of Social Work, & Anindita Bhattacharya, Columbia University dc3027@columbia.edu; el19@columbia.edu; ab4050@columbia.edu*

Depression disproportionately affects sexual minority men, yet few interventions exist for this population. To inform clinical interventions, the authors conducted a comprehensive meta-synthesis (Sandelowski, 2007) of sexual minority men's experiences with depression to: summarize current qualitative studies aims and findings; identify important gaps and limitations in this literature and understand patterns in clinical depression. We identified seven eligible peer-reviewed articles from Australia, United Kingdom and United States (published between 1998 and 2017). Their experiences included: a) perceived stressors (e.g., discrimination, marginalization); b) patterns of distress: followed a biomedical model; c) coping mechanisms (e.g., keeping depression secret, suicide, illicit drugs); and d) help seeking: men sought support from general practitioners who were perceived as empathic, humorous and provided a safe environment. Future work should explore diverse groups of sexual minority men (e.g., ethnic minority groups, older adults and non-English speakers). Implications for social work research and practice will be discussed.

1371373 **Assessing Physical and Mental Health Needs of Older Latino and African-American LGB Adults** *David Camacho, Columbia University; dc3027@columbia.edu*

By 2060, older Latinos and African-Americans will make up approximately 1/3rd (33 million) of the total US older adult population. Currently, 2-6% identify as lesbian, gay or bisexual (LGB). With the projected growth, the number of older Latino and African-American LGB adults will also increase significantly. To date, no studies have qualitatively explored their health needs. Thus, following CBPR principles this study qualitatively assesses physical and mental health needs of LGB older adults of color via three focus groups with community members and five semi-structured in depth interviews with their social services providers in New York. Preliminary results from our thematic analysis indicate that community members: face challenges in accessing medical care and adhering to treatment regimens, employ unique culturally-based self-management strategies, experience housing stressors resulting from being older and living with a same-sex partner, and receive critical social support from attending a safe and accepting senior social service program.

**The Uses of Theory in Case Study Research**<br>
*Kori Bloomquist, Winthrop University, Chair*<br>
Union 314 A

1383210 **Surveillance and Sousveillance: A Case Study of the Nervous CPS Worker** *Tara La Rose, McMaster University; larost1@mcmaster.ca*

Digital technologies give social workers new options and enhanced capacity for surveillance. The potential also exists to shift the power dynamics between clients and workers when clients also take up these technologies to create their own case recordings. These new forms of "veillance" are a reality that social workers and clients now work within, one which has received little attention from scholars and professional leaders. This paper seeks to consider these issues drawing on specific case-study example of surveillance and sousveillance using a publicly available YouTube video "The Nervous CPS Worker."

**1370545 Vietnamese College Students with Visual Impairments: A Qualitative Study of Their Experiences and Emotional Well-Being** *Tuyen Thi Thanh Bui, University of Illinois at Champaign-Urbana; ttbui2@illinois.edu*

**Introduction**: Visually impaired individuals face numerous challenges both at home and on campus. These challenges influence students F long-term well-being, educational and employment trajectories. This qualitative study is the first to explore these topics in Vietnam, a country that has a high percentage of visually impaired population. **Methods**: This multiple case-based study drew on in-depth interviews with 10 participants on their experiences at home and college, and on extensive field notes and informal observations of participants. Thematic-style analyses were undertaken to identify dominant and emergent themes and meaning units. **Results**: Challenges in secondary education that visually impaired students face include lack of accommodation from educational institutions, stigma and discrimination in childhood, and lack of awareness by the community about disability. **Implications**: Universities in Vietnam should have a special unit to provide support services for students with disabilities and organize activities to raise community awareness about people with disabilities.

**1374984 When Social Circus Trainers Put Themselves "at Disposal:" The Development of a Portrait Based on YouTube Videos and Mauss's Theory of the Gift** *Karin Hannes, Katholieke Universiteit Leuven; karin.hannes@kuleuven.be*

Social circus and leisure programs targeting vulnerable populations are increasingly recognized as a tool to alleviate the often distorted and disconnected relations some people experience, both on an individual level and an institutional level. These programs are delivered by social workers, circus professionals or both. It has been argued that those with a social welfare background are best equipped to guide people with challenging personal and life circumstances. This sparked our interest in what a social circus trainer should or could be. In a deliberate attempt to move away from the competence-based discourse that currently dominates discussions on what a good trainer should be, I turn to the theory of the gift from Marcel Mauss to illustrate the principle of giving, receiving, and rendering in the social bonding created between trainers and participants in their social circus universe.

**Problematizing the Resilience Discourse Within the Social Work Profession** *Ashley Prowell, The University of Alabama in Tuscaloosa; anprowell@crimson.ua.edu*

The literature defines resilience as being able to bounce back in the face of adversity. While the idea of resilience development is a tempting vision within several aspects of social work, resilience is also a political topic that invokes several questions and problems. On the surface, the current narrative of resilience is not an invalid one, yet the close consideration of marginalized groups in non-conducive environments produces an intricacy that can potentially be addressed by a more context-specific conceptualization of resilience. This paper proposes a systematic review that 1) examines the way in which social work professionals are currently conceptualizing resilience and 2) applies a poststructuralist lens to identify and improve the potential troubles that emerge from the current resilience discourse. Through this study, I hope to offer a more culturally candid perspective on risk and resilience and continuously improve thought and practice within social work education and research.

### 1373342 The Role of Social Capital in Fostering Resilience: A Sociological Perspective on Risk and Resilience

*Ashley Prowell, The University of Alabama in Tuscaloosa; anprowell@crimson.ua.edu*

The child poverty rate in the U.S. is among the highest of developed nations. Approximately one in five children in the U.S. live at or below the poverty line. The incidence of poverty experienced by ethnic minority youth has led to many becoming both economically and ethnically isolated. Resilience is a construct representing positive adaptation despite adversity. Echoed in the literature are several resilience factors that work to combat the effects of adversity, such as having a supportive adult relationship, but how can having supportive relationships potentially lead to more connectedness to the greater society? Drawing on Bourdieu's Sociological Model, the current study applies the concept of social capital (a hidden cause of inequality) and the role it plays in fostering resilience for at-risk youth. This case study explores the processes of accruing social capital through supportive adult relationships, eventually allowing youth to become active agents in the development of their resilience.

### 1370017 Adverse Childhood Experiences and The Social Environment: Interviews withWomen of Color

*Kori Bloomquist, Winthrop University, & Gabrielle Lee, Winthrop University; bloomquistk@winthrop.edu; leeg7@mailbox.winthrop.edu*

The term Adverse Childhood Experiences (ACEs) is used to describe many types of abuse, neglect, and trauma in childhood. Research demonstrates that ACEs are prevalent, however, sample diversity and examination of environmental and macro forces are often lacking in ACEs research. This study seeks to address gaps in ACEs research by asking: How do women of color describe the social environmental factors and experiences of their childhood? What role do adverse or traumatic childhood experiences within the social environment play in the lives of women of color? Five participants from a southeastern state completed the BRFSS ACEs scale and participated in in-depth, semi-structured interviews. Researchers used individual case descriptions, individual case analysis, and cross case analysis to identify transcendent themes and assertions. Findings indicate social pressures and protective factors in childhood and layered experiences related to race, class, gender, coping, and immediate and extended shaping forces.

### Cross-Cultural Meanings and Qualitative Approaches
*Festus Yaw Moasun, Wilfrid Laurier University, Chair*
Union 314 B

**1370817 Living with Stigma: Voices from the Cured Lepers Village in Southern Ghana** *Cynthia Akorfa Sottie, Booth University College, & Judith Kafui Darkey, Department of Social Welfare Ministry of Gender, Children and Social Protection Ghana cynthia_sottie@boothuc.ca; judithdarkey@yahoo.com*

Stigmatization of persons cured of leprosy (PCLs) is a long standing social problem especially in the developing world which often leads to their isolation from mainstream society. This study presents the voices of PCLs in the Cured Lepers' Village in Ho, a community located in Southern Ghana. The study collected data through in-depth interviews and focus group discussions with 20 participants. Findings indicate that PCLs make the Cured Lepers' Village their permanent home after they are cured of leprosy. This situation is as a result of the stigma, neglect, and isolation they experience. Fear of the disease which is fueled by ignorance, compliance with religious and socio-cultural beliefs, and regulations regarding leprosy were identified as reasons for the isolation of people affected by the disease. The study recommends a comprehensive public education program to demystify myths about leprosy, its causes and transmission.

**1370859 Kicking the Can Down the Road: Social Work Programs and Equivocation on the DACA Repeal** *Melissa Hardesty, Binghamton University, & Sarah Reta Young, Binghamton University; hardesty@binghamton.edu; syoung@binghamton.edu*

This study investigates the major themes in public messages released by social work programs in response to Trump's executive order to end the Deferred Action for Child Arrivals (DACA) program. We performed a Google search to identify DACA-related statements made by social work departments in the United States and coded any messages that appeared within the first 200 hits. Using the lens of the neoliberal university, we used open and thematic coding and found that: 1) Programs were far more likely to appeal to a higher university or professional authority than to articulate their own position on DACA, and 2) Most programs gave vague advice, if any, about how to respond to the repeal. Based on this initial analysis, we ask whether social work programs, situated in a neoliberal context, are motivated and resourced to take a strong public stand on political issues that directly implicate the social work profession.

1380526 **A Narrative Inquiry to Working Experiences of People with Hearing Impairment** *Min-Juan Wu, University of Taipei, Min-Chun Chiang, University of Taipei, & Li-chuan Kao, University of Taipei; w286girl@hotmail.com; dr.mirabear@gmail.com; lkao2006@gmail.com*

This inquiry was to explore the job search and work experiences of a person with hearing impairment who called Hua (a pseudonym). The data collection was based on narrative interviewing, and supplemented with file information and shadowing. With the narrative analysis as my research method, the participant's experiences and my reflections interweaved in the storytelling. The major conclusion is that all the hearing-impaired not only face difficulties because of deafness but also gains a lot in their career. In addition, through the interactions with the participant, I have been in self-reflection and aware of myself all the time, and I have lived a brilliant life with him. By this study, people with hearing impairment were more appreciable and understood in their work place. Moreover, I am looking forward to supporting them with great efforts more than before. It is looking forward to encouraging their ambitions in the coming future.

1374715 **The Power of the Tongue: Inherent Labeling of People with Disabilities in Proverbs of the Akans, Ghana** *Festus Yaw Moasun, Wilfrid Laurier University & Magnus Mfoafo-M'Carthy, Wilfrid Laurier University; moas3180@mylaurier.ca; mmfoafomcarthy@wlu.ca*

Proverbs are considered an important feature of any language worldwide. In Africa, proverbs are used in speech to add special effects. However, as a repository of African knowledge and culture, proverbs serve as a medium for educating present and future generations about society's cultural values, beliefs, and ethics. In this powerful role, proverbs may have very significant effects on speakers and their listeners. While these effects may be positive, in terms of their references to certain groups of people, proverbs may have telling effects on especially vulnerable populations. After examining a sample of Akan proverbs on mental and physical disabilities, this paper concludes that Akan proverbs predominantly label people with disability (PWDs) negatively, thereby leading to their stigmatisation, marginalisation, and exclusion. The paper recommends using proverbs with negative connotations for PWDs as a tool to educate society as to how not to treat PWDs.


**1:00-2:20**

**Concurrent Sessions**

1383182 **Workshop on Writing Articles for Publication**
*Sondra Fogel, University of South Florida, Editor of* Families in Society; *sfogel@usf.edu*
Union 210

Journal editors are concerned that many of the articles that PhD students and new professionals submit are not quite ready for a revise and re-submit, and so they are rejected. This workshop will be composed of journal editors and well-published researchers who will provide the nuts and bolts of writing up qualitative research. Topics include the various ways to open an article, components of the introductory sections, linking the introductory material to the rest of the article, what belongs in the methods and methodology section, ways of writing up results, and elements of the discussion.

1370380 Promoting the Implementation of Participatory Research Methods: Including Photovoice in Social Work Doctoral Curricula<br>
Susan Witte, ssw12@columbia.edu (Chair); Anindita Bhattacharya, ab4050@columbia.edu (Session Organizer); Carolina Velez-Grau, cmv2143@columbia.edu (Discussant); & David Camacho, dc3027@columbia.edu (Discussant)<br>
Union 314 A

This year's conference theme of "Qualitative Inquiry in Troubled Times" encourages social work to identify and implement innovative solutions to contemporary social problems. Initiated by doctoral students, the purpose of this symposium is to discuss the integration of CBPR methods, and particularly Photovoice, into doctoral curricula. As part of CBPR doctoral course in fall 2016, four doctoral students implemented three Photovoice projects with 1) refugee youth who have recently resettled in Lancaster, Pennsylvania; 2) adolescents receiving mental health services in New York City; and 3) Assertive Community Treatment (ACT) providers in New York City. The symposium includes presentation of the process and outcomes from each Photovoice project. We will discuss, from the perspectives of both doctoral students and faculty, lessons learned regarding the logistical challenges of taking on a Photovoice project and make recommendations regarding how best to incorporate Photovoice into all doctoral programs to advance pedagogical thinking in Critical Qualitative Inquiry.

Paper 1: Exploring Needs and Experiences of ACT Providers: A Photovoice Project

Paper 2: Adolescents' Perceptions of Mental Health: A Photovoice Project

Paper 3: Toward a More Client-Centered Evaluation of Integration: Findings from a Photovoice Project with Newly Arrived Refugee Youth in Lancaster, Pennsyvania

Qualitative Methods for Envisioning the Possible for Persons who Experience Social Exclusion<br>
Philip Young Hong, Loyola University Chicago, Chair<br>
Union 314 B

1370431 The Role of School Counselors in Promoting the Resilience of African American Adolescents from Urban Communities Alayna Ashley

Thomas, *North Carolina Agricultural and Technical State University;*
*aathomas@aggies.ncat.edu*

The purpose of this research is add to the existing knowledge on resilience and African American adolescents from urban communities. As a result of this study, one will be able to identify the roles of the family, school officials, the school counselor in promoting resilience in African American adolescents from urban communities. With such an understanding, family members, school officials, and counselors may be able to collaborate and advocate on behalf of African American adolescents in urban communities to help create change in the form of school policies, programs, and mental health services. Furthermore, the purpose of this current study is to identify the strategies that reinforce African American adolescents from urban communities patterns of resilience that allow adolescents to manage and cope with the problems and stressors associated with living in an urban community (Rak & Patterson, 1996).

### 1370474 Drawing for Interpretative Phenomenological Analysis: A Tool to Elicit and to Illustrate in Troubled Times? *Sarah Vicary, The Open University; sarah.vicary@open.ac.uk*

Drawing is used as a data generation tool in many areas of research including social work because it uses different cognitive processes. Drawing also provides an opportunity for researchers to access thoughts, feelings and emotions in different ways. In Interpretative Phenomenological Analysis (IPA) imaginative methods that allow such discovery, are encouraged. In the study which is the focus of this paper, one drawing method, Rich Pictures, was used in order to evoke thoughts and feelings in a way unfamiliar to participants, thereby allowing an opportunity to explore meaning that might otherwise be hidden. IPA was applied to verbatim texts that included the description of the participant's Rich Picture which were utilised, either whole or in part, to illustrate the findings. This paper will discuss whether this alone was the outcome or will question whether, for IPA, drawing can be used to elicit and illustrate data in troubled times?

### 1370762 Breakfast with Mr. Reasonable: Participatory Action Research and Autoethnography with Youth *Heather Murphy Sloane, University of Toledo; heather.sloane@utoledo.edu*

In answer to the interprofessional concern for better ways to teach students about difference, a program was initiated by social work faculty to bring university students from the professions to write with high school students from a large city school. Writing prompts are used to spark critical thinking and then each writer is provided strengths-based feedback. Professional and high school students learn about autoethnography and critical theory through these weekly sessions to explore the topic of social separation. Students observations give voice to youth unaccustomed to being heard. Working together as fellow researchers respect grows between participants for how we are all connected and separation based on class, race, and age begin to disappear. At this stage of the group the writing pieces will be brought together to analyze for themes and reach conclusions with the intent to develop a presentation proposal to be presented at a local social justice conference.

**1371637 Transforming Impossible to Possible (TIP) Talks: Wisdom for Humanship** *Philip Young Hong, Loyola University Chicago; phong@luc.edu*

The Transforming Impossible to Possible (TIP) program was developed by Dr. Philip Hong at Loyola University Chicago as a bottom-up model to empower low-income jobseekers in workforce development programs. The status quo job readiness training has faced many challenges as it typically focuses on the neoliberal model of "cleaning up" or "fixing up" the applicants to fit the taste of employers who control the labor market. TIP Talks is a resistance movement to challenge the inherent bias that there is something wrong with jobseekers "blaming the victim" for not being fully job ready and "employable." The narratives that represent TIP program participants as experts and providers of wisdom to the rest of the world shifts the power back to low-income jobseekers by demonstrating strength in humanship, defined as "leadership, in one's life or self-sponsorship through finding an optimal balance between awareness and action by focusing on one's internal locus of control" (Hong, 2016, p. 100).

**1371045 Sources of Strength in Transforming Impossible into Possible (TIP): Spiritual Perspectives of Low-Income Job Seekers** *Philip Young Hong, Loyola University Chicago, & Siddhesh Mukerji, Loyola University Chicago; phong@luc.edu; smukerji@luc.edu*

This paper presents spiritual perspectives on the experiences of low-income job seekers using a social work practice model called Transforming Impossible into Possible (TIP) as an applied example. TIP is an evidence-informed practice model that strengthens psychological self-sufficiency (PSS) in the context of goal setting and achievement. Low-income job seekers PSS barriers and hope can be understood not only through the lens of current social science theory, but also through the constructs found in spiritual traditions. Thus, the authors describe how Biblical perspectives of selfless, unconditional, and sacrificial love towards which faith and hope exert motivational strength necessary to conquer individual and structural barriers. The authors then examine the experience of low-income job seekers using the Buddhist *paramitas,* or transcendent practices, of diligence, patience, meditation, wisdom, morality, and generosity. The authors posit that concepts from spiritual traditions can serve as an effective lens for qualitative inquiry into the human experience.

**Qualitative Interviewing and the Concerns of Children and Youth**
*Jonel Thaller, Ball State University, Chair*
Union 404

**1371333 Stress Coping Experiences Among American Parents of Children with Comorbid ADHD and Autism** *Jinhee Koo, University at Albany; jkoo2@albany.edu*

This phenomenological study aims to develop a preliminary understanding of stress coping experiences among American parents of children with comorbid attention deficit hyperactive disorder (ADHD) and autism. A descriptive and exploratory study design was used. Three mothers of children with comorbid ADHD and autism were recruited through snowball sampling in Albany, NY. All three mothers held graduate degrees. Data were collected through brief demographic questionnaires and semi-structured interviews. Manifest and latent content analysis were employed with open and axial coding procedures. The researcher's personal journal and analytic memos supported the analysis. Parents' stress coping experiences emerged as moving from out of control to under control, showing a gradual development of adaptive coping over time. Additionally, the role of the mothers' educational background emerged as a theme. Findings contribute to understanding well educated mothers' stress coping experiences and can inform future studies, including potential comparisons with less educated parents.

### 1369250 An Exploration of Ethnic and Cultural Identity for Multiracial Individuals Adopted Transracially *Stephen T. Wilson, University of Washington; wilsonst@uw.edu*

This retrospective and exploratory study interviewed eleven individuals, who identified as biracial or multiracial, and were adopted transracially into White homes. The goal of this study was to gain an understanding of their voiced experiences in receiving support for their racial and ethnic identities. Interviews focused on self and other identification experiences, identifying challenging life situations, and where and whether identity crises may have occurred. The researcher also sought out information on how key informants garnered supports to reclaim a viable sense of him/her self as a person of color, while living in a White home or community as a transracially adopted youth. These narratives will add to the thinking about transracial adoptees' experiences. The narratives will also inform parents and social workers in supporting multiracial children to explore their ethnic identities. In addition, the study will help normalize multiracial individuals' life experiences as transracial adoptees.

### 1389694 Do Inpatient Substance Use Clients Fit the Emerging Adulthood Theoretical Cookie Cutter Characteristics? *Kelly Lynn Clary, University of Illinois at Urbana-Champaign, & Douglas Cary Smith, University of Illinois at Urbana-Champaign; valenck2@illinois.edu; smithdc@illinois.edu*

The purpose of this qualitative study was to uncover emerging adults' impressions of the theory on emerging adults. Participants were 18-29 years old (female =7, male = 14) who completed at least 30 days in an inpatient substance abuse treatment center in a Midwestern state. The results help recognize the perspectives of a highly-marginalized group of people and expands research of Jeffrey Arnett's (2000) Emerging Adulthood framework. Participants completed an in-person interview that uncovered their thoughts and experiences of the 5 characteristics, "identity exploration, instability, self-focus, feeling in between adolescence and adulthood, and optimism about the future." Audio recordings were transcribed, analyzed in NVivo and coded. Focus groups were held to assist with member checking. Analysis of the main themes revealed that most participants related to the expected features. Major overarching themes include freedom, spectrum of responsibilities, influence of background experiences, and using substances to cope with unsettled emotions.

**1371088 Youth Homelessness and Geographic Mobility: Neoliberal Policy, Service Gaps, and System Limitations** *Amanda Aykanian, University at Albany; amanda.aykanian@gmail.com*

This qualitative study began as a phenomenological exploration of providers' experiences working with geographically mobile homeless youth. It evolved into a critical discussion, between researcher and participants, about restrictive policies, service and capacity limitations, and engagement challenges faced when working with highly mobile youth in a geographically-diverse region. In-depth interviews were conducted with eight homeless service providers in New York's Capital Region. The analysis centered on perceptions of mobility and how policy and service system factors impact mobility. Participants described mobility as an impulsive coping strategy, a process greatly influenced by service system and policy limitations, and a phenomenon that challenges traditional engagement strategies. Findings suggest opportunities for strengthening the service system through trauma-informed programming and policy, increased coordination with government and other policy-making entities, and assessing gaps in key services. Implications and recommendations are presented with special attention to the role of social workers and the social work profession.

**1371589 Adolescent Development and Sex Trafficking: The Role of Adult Caregivers and Service Providers in Entry and Exit** *Jonel Thaller, Ball State University, Andrea Cimino, Johns Hopkins University, Rachel Keeney, Johns Hopkins University, & Alexis Kennedy, University of Nevada Las Vegas;* jthaller@bsu.edu; acimino2@jhu.edu; rachelkeeney@jhu.edu; alexis.kennedy@unlv.edu

As part of healthy adolescent development, teenagers naturally take risks and distance themselves from their adult caregivers as they transition into independence. Teenaged girls from supportive families often "play" at adulthood before they embark, whereas others may be prematurely propelled into adulthood, encountering predatory adults who capitalize upon their adolescent minds and bodies by involving them in domestic minor sex trafficking (DMST). In interviews with young women commercially sexually exploited as youth (n=40), we examined how typical adolescent developmental tasks influenced their entry into and exit from commercial sexual exploitation (CSE). Many youth recalled being lured into CSE by promise of financial independence or love and acceptance. Many also reported they had been reluctant to comply with supportive adult caregivers or service providers, in part because they felt ashamed or misunderstood, and they implored adults to be open-minded and persevering when working with challenging adolescents because positive growth is possible.

**1370807 Visual Storytelling: Decolonizing Social Work Practice** *Natalie St-Denis, University of Calgary, & Christine Walsh, University of Calgary; nstdeni@ucalgary.ca; cwalsh@ucalgary.ca*

The profession of social work has an historical and ongoing role in the oppression of Indigenous peoples, and, consequently has the responsibility to honour Indigenous worldviews in its endeavours. Storytelling, described as an embodiment of Indigenous knowledges, validates the experiences of Indigenous peoples. Further, visual methods of storytelling have gained popularity among oppressed communities as way to share their experiences. Photography has been established as a qualitative research methodology in the social sciences to evoke emotional reactions and awareness about social conditions with the purpose of influencing and directly impacting social and policy changes. This photo-story was developed to support social work students in decolonizing their practice by reflecting on their personal and professional identities in relationship to place. In this presentation we make the invisible visible through a series of evocative images and invite the audience to consider their identities as embedded in historical, cultural and structural realities.

**1371323 Teachers, Trauma, and the Classroom: Investigating Trauma Training for Working with Syrian Refugee Students** *Christine Mayor, Wilfrid Laurier University; mayo6830@mylaurier.ca*

Previous research demonstrates the impact of traumatic exposure on refugee students' learning, with the school increasingly seen as an appropriate and necessary place for trauma identification and intervention. Yet, this research has often left out the classroom experiences of teachers, despite them spending the most time with students. This qualitative study focuses on teachers' experiences of applying trauma training to the classroom when teaching Syrian refugee children. This research highlights specific examples of how trauma "emerges' in the classroom, including data about what situations teachers continue to struggle with despite being given training. Implications for how social workers might support teachers in trauma-informed classrooms will be articulated, as well as the potential need to re-consider what content and through what method teachers are provided this training.

**1383878 Positive Discrimination as Discourse: A Methodological Approach for Studying Australian and Chilean Experiences. First Part** *Vanessa Jara-Labarth, University of Tarapacç, & Cesar Cisneros-Puebla, Autonomous Metropolitan University, Iztapalapa; vanedk@gmail.com; cesar41_4@hotmail.com*

In this essay I will describe the conceptual and methodological basis for an ongoing empirical project conducted in Arica - Chile, that explores the challenges indigenous students are facing in higher education. A narrative autobiographical approach has been implemented to analyze the indigenous legacy's impact in their academic trajectories. As social worker I am interested in propose a framework to generate public policies and social awareness about indigenous way of living within Chilean higher education. This report is a preliminary international presentation of our methodological approach based on a very specific Australian and Chilean experiences description.

### 1383917 Positive Discrimination as Discourse: A Methodological Approach for Studying Australian and Chilean Experiences. Second Part

*Cesar Cisneros-Puebla, Autonomous Metropolitan University, Iztapalapa, & Vanessa Jara-Labarth, University of Tarapacç; cesar41_4@hotmail.com; vanedk@gmail.com*

The second part of this project presents some of the findings we are analyzing using Sch∫tze's narrative autobiographical approach. Nowadays, there are many debates about the disciplinary field of Social Work, mainly within Chilean universities, and from our perspective, through this kind of qualitative research, we are aiming to demonstrate that, methodologically speaking, it is possible to integrate advanced and rigorous ways of researching lived experiences to the Social Work practices within the Chilean academic context. In addition, this humble effort seeks to become a contribution to produce useful knowledge in the Chilean society.

**2:30-3:50**

### Concurrent Sessions

### 1383224 Roundtable: Toward Social Work Specific Research: The Legacy of the Chicago School of Sociology

*Jane F. Gilgun, University of Minnesota; Jim Drisko, Smith College; & Nicole Corley, Virginia Commonwealth University;*
*jgilgun@umn.edu; jdrisko@smith.edu; ncorley@vcu.edu*
Union 210

Social work has struggled to develop research methods and methodologies that are specific to the discipline. Approaches originating within the Chicago School of Sociology can further this development. In fact, the research methods of the Chicago School of Sociology could be named The Chicago School of Social Work Research because members of the Hull House settlement were early contributors to the Chicago School not only in terms of understanding social problems and crafting policies and programs, but also in terms of research methods and methodologies that later became known as grounded theory, deductive qualitative analysis, and fieldwork. They also contributed to symbolic interactionism and American pragmatism, both associated with social work and sociology. The format includes a presentation (Gilgun), a response (Drisko), a reflection panel (Nicole & one other volunteer), and dialogue with all present.

1370132 **Workshop: Transcendent Reentry:
Successful Transition Experience of Citizens Returning from Prison**
*Thomas Kenemore, Loyola University Chicago, & Brent In, Loyola University Chicago;
thomas@kenemore.org; brentin8737@gmail.com*
Union 404

Reentry from prison or jail to community, along with other issues in the troubled criminal justice system, is politicized, not well understood, and largely ignored by those in power. In particular, the voices of returning citizens are essentially unheard. Several years of qualitative inquiry into their experiences, from a wide range of perspectives, has produced a thematic look into the factors essential for successful reentry, defined by those experiencing the process. The transition from incarceration to freedom is an extremely challenging and torturous journey from a highly controlled and dangerous ecological surround to a highly uncontrolled and dangerous environment. Our research in this black box of reentry process has revealed some transcendent intrapersonal and relational factors that are essential to self-defined reentry success. We will share these thematic descriptions and discuss how they can inform practitioners and organizations committed to advocating for, and working with, this vastly underserved population.

## Intersectionality and Women's Experiences
*Kelly Munly, Penn State Altoona, Chair*
Union 314 A

1370642 **Intersectionality: A Theoretical Lens to Better Understand Domestic Violence among Immigrants, University of Alabama** *Burcu Ozturk,
University of Alabama, & Debra Nelson-Gardell, University of Alabama;
bozturk@crimson.ua.edu; dnelsong@sw.ua.edu*

Intersectionality theory allows social workers to analyze the oppressions faced by women, especially nonwhite women, in the United States. The fundamental insight from intersectionality theory involves observation of how social categories, by which hierarchies are formed, affects individuals (Marecek,2016). Intersectional analysis describing battered women's oppression illuminates intensification through the aspects of race, ethnicity, class, gender, sexual orientation, and immigrant status to systems of oppression and discrimination (Marecek, 2016). Since 1990, the gender of recent immigrant populations has altered, intensifying the problem of domestic violence in immigrant communities (Ammar & Orloff, 2005; Sokoloff, 2008). Understanding the intersectionality of race, class, gender, marginalization, oppression and discrimination and how the intersections influence domestic violence in the lives of immigrant women holds importance (Sokoloff, 2008). The central purpose of this intentionally interactive presentation will focus on discussion with and contributions from conference attendees enhancing all of our understandings of this aspect of oppression.

1371372 **Listening to Women's Stories of Institutionalization and Community Reintegration: A Feminist Narrative Inquiry** *Anindita Bhattacharya, Columbia University, & Ellen Lukens, Columbia University School of Social Work; ab4050@columbia.edu; el19@columbia.edu*

In India, various underlying structural factors (e.g. gender discrimination, poverty, interpersonal violence, family abandonment and legal loopholes in mental health laws) serve to keep women with serious mental illness (SMI) isolated in psychiatric institutions. Despite this, narratives of women with SMI and their needs and experiences have not received much visibility in mental health research. Using a feminist narrative inquiry, my dissertation highlights the socio-political realities of women with SMI at a half way home in Kolkata, India. I examine how women's narratives are shaped by gender and their social positioning. Women share accounts related to contextual factors that contributed to their illness and admission to mental hospital(s) and their experiences reintegrating with the community following prolonged institutionalization. This study includes ethnographic methods to investigate how social, cultural, and institutional discourses surrounding gender and mental health impact service delivery at the half way home.

1369919 **Troubling Social Work Intervention in Situations of Domestic Violence** *Beth Archer-Kuhn, University of Calgary, & Caitlin Harris, University of Calgary; beth.archerkuhn@ucalgary.ca; caitlin.harris@ucalgary.ca*

The prevalence of families who are impacted by domestic violence in Alberta is staggering and continues to grow. Researchers note that organizations providing services to families who have experienced violence often lack the necessary information to effectively support families; specifically, women are held to a high standard in the protection of their children. Similarly, research recommends the need to engage professionals to increase their understanding of the linkages between masculinity and domestic violence. In this phenomenological study, seven child protective services workers help us to understand their experience of a curriculum training program. Utilizing thematic analysis, the findings from this study begin a dialogue that challenges the types of professional development and training that are required to work in this very demanding field. The study identifies one way in which phenomenology helps to identify social justice concerns for survivors of violence through the experiences of child protection workers.

1381153 **Autoethnography: Immersion** *Kelly Munly, Penn State Altoona, & Jai Mitchell; kam6832@psu.edu; jaifilms@gmail.com*

This autoethnography offers a bricolage of research analysis, reflective narrative and illustration and is meant to evoke a more holistic vision of individuals who may otherwise be othered for reasons of age or disability. We hope that you take inspiration from this work to your own community contexts to improve conditions for older adults and adults living with disabilities. Ageism and ableism limit opportunities and consequently create obstacles for reasonable quality of life. As a democracy, we should be vigilant to be conscious and intentional about providing equal opportunity for all. Equal opportunity requires being vigilant about overcoming misunderstandings about cognitive decline and other mental and physical health challenges often associated with older age and disability. All individuals deserve to be treated as whole and equal.

### Insider Perspectives and Qualitative Research

*Paul A. Maxfield, Kansas State University: Chair*
Union 314 B

**1375134 A Qualitative Data Analysis: Family Victim Advocates in Child Advocacy Centers** *Teresa L Young, Texas A&M University Kingsville, Quentin R Maynard, University of Alabama Tuscaloosa, & Bethany Womack, University of Tennessee Chattanooga; teresa.young@tamuk.edu; qrmaynard@crimson.ua.edu; bethany-womack@utc.edu*

Family victim advocates in child advocacy centers provide a valuable resource to children and parents involved in child abuse investigations. This work requires family victim advocates be knowledgeable in such areas as child development, crisis intervention, community resources, family relationships, and child welfare and criminal justice systems. The current study reports the findings from a survey of family victim advocates employed in child advocacy centers related to their motivation for doing the work as well as their perceptions of their training and potential training needs. A group of doctoral students comprised the research team and worked collaboratively under the supervision of university faculty to conduct the qualitative data analysis. The findings describe the characteristics and motivations of family victim advocates working in child advocacy centers and emphasize the need for more advanced trainings that focus on skill-building and strengths-based practices utilized to support children and parents in child abuse cases.

**1371620 What Makes Refugees Want to Participate in Resettlement Programs or Services? Insider Perspectives** *An Thi Ha, University of Utah, College of Social Work; hathiansw@gmail.com*

As they adjust to host societies and new cultures, refugees have experienced significant challenges and at the same time, demonstrated resiliency in resettlement. In the route of seeking a "best practice" for resettling and integrating these diverse, vulnerable population, community participation, a bottom-up, community-driven approach, is considered an alternative of failed top-down, expertise-led development strategy. This approach is seen as a crucial component to build a strong community which enhances and appreciates active engagement of all community members. Why people participate and what encourages their participation? Reasons and factors motivating an individual, a group or a community participate in a program are various based on their own characteristics. This paper will discuss motivational factors in community participation among various refugee backgrounders through a pilot research project.

**1383778 Researching Norms, Narratives, and Transforming Sexuality: The Importance of Women's Art-Therapy Focus Groups in Contemporary China** *Yuxin Pei, Sun Yat-Sen University; peisysu@qq.com*

Through interviews with 118 women in 10 art-therapy focus groups, we explored norms and narratives of sexuality. We found that this type of focus group led to spontaneous self-disclosure. Participants discovered taken-for-granted norms of women's sexuality and built new narratives about unspoken, inexplicit, or hidden past experiences. Women' s active, participative, and receptive arts engagement for self-expressions are also examined.

**1370930 The Meaning of Living-Apart-Together in Continuing Care Retirement Communities: Perspectives of Residents and Healthcare Professionals** *Chaya Koren University of Haifa, & Liat Ayalon, Bar Ilan University; ckoren@univ.haifa.ac.il; liat.ayalon@biu.ac.il*

Late-life repartnering and the move to a continuing care retirement community (CCRC) are relatively new occurrences associated with the process of modernization representing new beginnings in old age. How these occurrences co-constitute each other has yet to be studied. We aim to examine how late-life repartnering and living in a CCRC social environment interact and are co-constituted from perspectives of residents and healthcare professionals. Thirty semi-structured qualitative interviews were conducted in three CCRCs in Israel; ten with repartnered residents, ten with residents not repartnered and ten with healthcare professionals. Two themes emerged: 1. Friendship rather than partnership; 2. Not living together yet being all the time together. A person-in-environment approach is used for discussing the construction of repartnered relationships in CCRCs as exclusive friendships and the limited autonomy as a consequence of not living together yet being all the time together. Implications on micro, mezzo and macro levels are suggested.

**1370811 Re-storying Couples in Sobriety: Using Qualitative Inquiry to Humanize Relationships in Recovery** *Paul A. Maxfield, Kansas State University; pmaxfield@ksu.edu*

Addiction is often associated with social discourses of shame, trauma, destruction, manipulation, and hopelessness. These stigmas can produce barriers for individuals seeking treatment and maintaining sobriety, as well as for the maintenance of partnerships and families. The narratives of recovery are challenged by the potential for relapse, and fear of a return to problem-saturated storylines of addiction. Significant others who stay in relationships with addicts are frequently depicted as weak and enabling. Couples with a partner in recovery lack positive models for sustaining their relationships throughout their journeys from active addiction to long-term recovery. This presentation will investigate the ways in which a couple in long-term recovery have re-storied their experiences with alcoholism through recovery in order to create positive and affirming narratives of themselves as individuals, and of their relationship. This re-storying process challenges prevailing Western social discourses around relationships in addiction and recovery.

**1372658 Child Abuse Mandatory Reporting: Perspectives of Israeli-Arab Art-Therapists** *Zakiah Massarwa, YAHAT, & Guy Enosh, University of Haifa; zakiah02@gmail.com; enosh@research.haifa.ac.il*

The purpose of the study was to observe the difficulties faced by Israeli-Arab art therapists when faced with an indication of reasonable suspicion that the client has experienced abuse. Such therapists are faced with conflicting loyalties and priorities. The best-interests-of-the-child; mandated-reporting; social expectations from family, colleagues, superiors, and community adhering to collectivist-norms. The cultural gap between the state's law and the conservative patriarchal Arab society; the potential outcomes of reporting for child client well-being; the potential reactions of the child's family and the community; all those are issues that a therapist has to take into account and weighs while facing the dilemma of mandatory reporting. Based on in-depth interviews with twelve therapists. Six central themes were derived: Professional practice; reactions following reporting; doubts concerning reporting; the client and the therapeutic process and the therapeutic relationship; professional difficulties vs. personal values; and, the society and community where participants live.

**1372637 Working with Resistances to Research within Protective Bureaucracy: A Case Description and Analysis** *Guy Enosh, University of Haifa, & Tali Bayer-Topilsky, Myers-JDC-Brokdale; enosh@research.haifa.ac.il; talit@jdc.org*

Child-protective services around the globe are reported to have an over-representation of minority groups. Previous research has indicated an inherent bias in child-placement recommendations by social workers working in the child-protective-services of Israel. The Ministry of Welfare (MoW) research department has decided to order a replication study which would examine the group decision making processes as occurring within the "committees for treatment and planning" that actually make the decision regarding the treatment plan and placement recommendations. The current presentation will attempt to describe in concise terms a process of more than two years of meeting, negotiating, discussing and reforming the proposed research in light of the perspectives of the different stakeholders. The key was to attempt to understand the related concerns, and work away from a position of etic researchers coming to do research on the committees, to an emic position of a researcher coming to do research with all involved.

**1380908 Gender Differences in a Child Advocacy Center** *Jill C Schreiber, Southern Illinois University Edwardsville, & Taylor Dichsen, Sothern Illinois University, Edwardsville; jischre@siue.edu; tdichse@siue.edu*

In this mixed methods study, 2016 and 2017 case data from the Madison County Child Advocacy Center (CAC) was analyzed for possible differences between male and female child abuse victims. The data included victim and perpetrator demographics as well as case details, such as outcome and officials involved. Males made up a majority of the victims abused by perpetrators within the home, while females were the majority of victims abused by perpetrators outside the home. In addition, as victim age group increased, the proportion of male victims decreased while the proportion of female victims increased. These results were presented to the CAC's multi-disciplinary team, and an interview with the team was conducted regarding possible explanations and implications of the findings. By identifying differences in the experiences of male and female child abuse victims, CACs can better interview them, social service workers can better aid them, and communities can better support them

1371350 **Preparing for Foster Children** *Jill C Schreiber, Southern Illinois University Edwardsville, Anna Mae Wells, Southern Illinois University Edwardsville, & Caroline Barrettsmart, Southern Illinois University Edwardsville; jischre@siue.edu; annwell@siue.edu; cabarre@siue.edu*

Foster families experience a variety of challenges during the initial placement process. Their ability to successfully navigate these challenges depends on their overall preparedness and access to formal and informal resources. Through surveys and interviews, foster parents reported that they received formal resources in the form of child welfare involvement, professional counseling, or community programs. Informal resources came from helpful community or extended family members, the foster child's school, and/or support from the church community. Other foster parents reported feeling unprepared. Implications include ways that workers can better prepare and support foster family creation, which could improve foster family placement stability and improve relationships between foster children and parents.

1371337 **Foster Parent Religiosity** *Jill C Schreiber, Southern Illinois University Edwardsville, Janet Wiley, Southern Illinois University Edwardsville, Rachel Schweitzer, Southern Illinois University Edwardsville, & Taylor Dichsen, Southern Illinois University Edwardsville; jischre@siue.edu; jlwiley1999@gmail.com; raschwe@siue.edu; tdichse@siue.edu*

Foster parents strive to provide a safe, stable environment for the children they bring into their homes. Many foster parents are motivated by religious values to become foster parents. Foster children often have histories of abuse and neglect that can lead to externalizing behaviors. Affiliation with religious communities could support foster parents by providing them purpose and meaning as well as social and material support. Religion can also provide the foster children a sense of belonging in the greater religious community. However, dissimilar levels or types of religiosity could provide conflict between foster parents and children. Through surveys and interviews current foster parents reported that religious practices are important to them. They described specific religious practices they had in their homes and their participation in religious communities. They also reported that the foster children in their home willingly became involved in the religion of the family.

**Plenary Session**

**Town Hall Meeting**
**Reflections on Social Work Day and What's Next**
*Jane F. Gilgun, University of Minnesota, Chair*

5:30-6:30                                                              Illini Room A

**Tea & Coffee Reception Illini Union**

**A Chance to Mingle**
**All are Welcome**

7:00-9:00

**Midwest Barbeque**